PRAISE FOR

It's So Amazing!

An American Library Association Notable Children's Book
A Cooperative Children's Book Center Choice Title
A *Children's Literature* Choice List Title
A *Horn Book Magazine* Fanfare Title

"Reassuring and warm . . . it's hard to imagine a more sensitive treatment than in these pages. The text recognizes children's feelings and fears, and reassures, line by line, that they are always lovable and always loved, no matter what. Beyond biology, *It's So Amazing!* is finally about love, and that, we hope, is where babies come from."
—*New York Times*

"Even if your child hasn't reached puberty, talk with him or her about what lies ahead. If you'd like some help, check out the excellent picture book *It's So Amazing!* by Robie Harris and Michael Emberley. . . . It could help prepare your son or daughter—as well as reassure you." —*Time* Magazine

★ "The author and illustrator duo that broke new ground with their frank talk and depiction of puberty and changing bodies in *It's Perfectly Normal* (1994) returns with an equally outstanding book. . . . Meets the needs of those in-between or curious kids who are not ready, developmentally or emotionally, for *It's Perfectly Normal.*"
—*Booklist* (starred review)

◆ "Harris and Emberley fill the gap between their picture book *Happy Birth Day!* (1996) and the instant-classic *It's Perfectly Normal* (1994) with this equally sensitive, good-humored take on love and sex, puberty, genetics, pregnancy, and related topics from sibling rivalry to HIV."
—*Kirkus Reviews* (pointered review)

★ "Parents looking for a way to keep embarrassment to a minimum when discussing sexuality with their young children will appreciate this book."
—*The Horn Book* (starred review)

★ "Another barrier-breaking contribution by Harris and Emberley that seamlessly bridges *It's Perfectly Normal* and *Happy Birth Day!* . . . An essential guide that will delight and inform and appeal to young readers as well as adults."
—*School Library Journal* (starred review)

PRAISE FROM THE EXPERTS

"This thoughtful, innovative, and comprehensive book helps children with issues that are on their minds anyway—and gives all of us the language we need to share with them."
—T. Berry Brazelton, MD, founder of Brazelton Touchpoints Center, Boston Children's Hospital, and Joshua Sparrow, MD, co-authors of *Touchpoints: Birth to Three* and *Touchpoints: Three to Six*

"With their deep appreciation for the perspectives and feelings of young children, the author and illustrator have discovered a powerful way to teach the complicated facts of life. Weaving together information about healthy sexuality—including how babies are made and develop, what makes us female or male, growing bodies, all kinds of families, and keeping safe—this wonderful book promotes learning and knowledge while helping to insure our children's physical and emotional health. It's so amazing that there is now a book for children and families that addresses so many of the questions that are so difficult to ask and discuss!"
—Steven Marans, MSW, PhD, Professor of Child Psychiatry and Psychiatry, Director of Childhood Violent Trauma Center, Yale University School of Medicine Child Study Center

"An excellent resource on sex education for young children, presented in a lively and engaging style for both kids and parents. A book every family should own."
—Alvin F. Poussaint, MD, Professor of Psychiatry, Harvard Medical School; co-author of *Raising Black Children: Two Leading Psychiatrists Confront the Educational, Social and Emotional Problems Facing Black Children*

"As a pediatrician, I know that children have many questions about reproduction, birth, bodies, babies, and families. Finding the answers, in a comfortable, appropriate, and interesting way, is an essential part of growing up healthy in body and mind. This book provides an opportunity for children to find answers to their questions with clarity of explanation, fabulous illustrations, and humor, together with an all-important sense of wonder." —Perri Klass, MD, Professor of Journalism and Pediatrics, New York University

"The array of enthusiastic fans *It's So Amazing!* has garnered is remarkable. Why do elementary-school children, along with parents, teachers, librarians, health professionals, community organizers, and clergy find the information about sexuality in this book so fascinating, appealing, and informative? Because Harris and Emberley have caringly created a book that is accurate, funny, clear, honest, up-to-date, and child-friendly. It not only educates children about sexuality, but it also provides the reassurance adults need to answer children's questions with confidence. And it opens up family discussions about values and the importance of sexual health. This is a must-have book." —Martha M. Walz, President and Chief Executive Officer, Planned Parenthood League of Massachusetts

A Note to the Reader
Celebrating the 15th Anniversary Edition of
It's So Amazing!

One of the most amazing science stories is how an egg and sperm get together to make a baby. While creating this book, both of us were fascinated by this story of how we all began. And we bet that you would be fascinated too.

Ever since this book was first published fifteen years ago, we have continued to talk with kids and adults about the information in it. And we've found out that today's kids, parents, teachers, librarians, and health professionals continue to think that the information in this book is so amazing! Over the years, another exciting thing has happened: every year, this book is used in more and more countries around the world.

Kids everywhere have lots of questions about how girls' and boys' bodies are the same and how they are different, about how babies are made, and about how kids' bodies grow and change. However, information about these topics often can and does change. So for this fifteenth anniversary edition, we asked parents, teachers, librarians, doctors, nurses, psychologists, psychoanalysts, scientists, and clergy what needed to be changed or added to *It's So Amazing!* And we spent a lot of time talking to and checking with these experts to make sure that all the information in this anniversary edition is as scientifically accurate and as up-to-date as possible. When we learned that new information or a new topic or new art needed to be included, we added it. That's why we have added more information about being online and using the Internet to this newest edition of our book.

We hope that you will find the information in our newest edition as amazing and fascinating as both of us still do today. We also hope that *It's So Amazing!* will continue to answer most of the questions you may have about eggs, sperm, girls, boys, bodies, love, pregnancy, birth, babies, adoption, and families. But if you have more questions about any information in our book, it can also be very helpful to talk with someone you know and trust— a parent, doctor, nurse, teacher, librarian, therapist, school counselor, or clergy member—and even share *It's So Amazing!* with that person.

Robie H. Harris and Michael Emberley

For Elaine Markson

Second edition 2014

The Library of Congress has cataloged the hardcover edition as follows:

Harris, Robie H.
It's so amazing! / a book about eggs, sperm, birth, babies, and families /
Robie H. Harris ; illustrated by Michael Emberley. —1st ed.
p. cm.
Includes index.
Summary: Uses bird and bee cartoon characters to present straightforward explanations of topics related to sexual development, love, reproduction, adoption, sexually transmitted diseases, and more.
ISBN 978-0-7636-0051-8 (first hardcover edition)
ISBN 978-0-7636-6873-0 (second hardcover edition)
1. Human reproduction—Juvenile literature. 2. Sex instruction for children—Juvenile literature.
[1. Human reproduction. 2. Sex instruction for children.] I. Emberley, Michael, ill. II. Title.
QP251.5.H37 1999
612.6—dc21   98-33119

ISBN 978-0-7636-1321-1 (first paperback edition)
ISBN 978-0-7636-6874-7 (second paperback edition)

16 17 18 19 20 APS 10 9 8 7 6 5

Printed in Humen, Dongguan, China

This book was typeset in ITC Bookman and Providence Sans Educational.
The illustrations were done in colored pencil and watercolor.

Candlewick Press
99 Dover Street
Somerville, Massachusetts 02144

visit us at www.candlewick.com

IT'S SO AMAZING!

A Book about Eggs, Sperm, Birth, Babies, and Families

Robie H. Harris

illustrated by
Michael Emberley

CANDLEWICK PRESS

CONTENTS

MEET THE BIRD AND THE BEE
Do You Know What I Read?

① CURIOUS? EMBARRASSED? CONFUSED?

So How Do Babies Really Begin?

Have you ever looked at your baby pictures?

Have you ever wondered where babies come from—or how babies are made—or where you came from—or how you really began?

Everyone—grandparents, parents, sisters, brothers, cousins, aunts, uncles, friends, and even teachers, firefighters, librarians, gymnasts, astronauts, dentists, scientists, cooks, nurses, shopkeepers, doctors, bus drivers, pilots, police officers, hockey players, mayors, and rock stars—every person in the whole wide world was a baby once. The arrival of a new baby is so amazing! Most kids—but not all—are curious about how such an amazing and wonderful thing could possibly happen.

You may think that by now you already know—or that you should know—exactly how a baby is made. But even if your mom or dad has talked to you about this, or even if you and your friends have talked about it—it's still perfectly normal to have questions about where babies come from. Talking with a parent, a doctor, a nurse, or a teacher is a good way to find out answers to your questions. And if you are thinking of using a computer or tablet to go online (on the Internet), ask any of these grown-ups to help you find a safe site for kids where you can get information about questions you may have or topics you may be interested in, such as how our bodies work and grow or how babies begin.

I'm so glad it's normal to have questions about THAT!

I have questions about dinosaurs— about outer space— but NOT about babies!

Sometimes you may feel very private about your questions and thoughts and feelings about how babies begin. Or it may feel embarrassing or hard to ask questions about making babies. Feeling curious about this, or embarrassed, or private, or even confused, is perfectly normal. And having lots of questions about where babies come from is also perfectly normal.

Since the beginning of time, people young and old have tried to figure out where babies come from and how a baby is made. But how a baby is made is not a simple thing. That's why learning about it can be interesting and even fun— no matter how old you are.

I can't WAIT to find out more about this!

I CAN wait.

EGG + SPERM = BABY

Reproduction

When a new baby animal or plant is made, scientists call that "reproduction." To reproduce means "to make again"— to make the same thing again.

Reproduction is how plants and animals make new plants and animals like themselves.

One fact about making a human baby is quite simple. It takes a sperm and an egg to make a baby.

What's so simple about THAT?

EGG + SPERM = BABY! THAT is simple addition!

Sperm and eggs are cells. In fact, all plants and animals—including humans—are made up of cells. And the human body is made up of millions and millions and millions of cells.

It says here, "There are brain cells, skin cells, bone cells, muscle cells, egg cells, sperm cells—and all sorts of other kinds of cells." Now, THAT'S amazing!

It says here, "There are about 200 different kinds of cells in the human body." Now, THAT'S science!

Hmmm . . . "An egg cell is one of the largest cells in the human body."

Ahhh . . . but did you know that a sperm cell is one of the smallest cells in the human body?

Sperm and eggs are the cells that can make a baby. The beginning cells of many animals—but not all—start to grow when an egg cell joins together with a sperm cell. This is the way humans make new babies. In fact, the beginning cells of a human baby can start to grow *only* when a sperm cell and an egg cell have joined together.

SAME AND DIFFERENT
Male Bodies—Female Bodies

Another fact that's quite simple is that human babies and most other animals are born female or male. Girls and women are called female. Boys and men are called male.

Most parts of our bodies—our toes, our fingers, our noses, our legs, our arms, our eyes, our hearts, our lungs, our stomachs, our buttocks—are the same and look quite the same whether we are born female or male.

SAME

SAME

SAME

DIFFERENT

Some of the private parts we are born with are not the same. The vagina and the penis are two of these private parts that are not the same for females and males. Some of our private parts are on the outside of our bodies and some are inside our bodies. Some are also the parts—when a person's body grows up—that can make a baby.

SAME

A male's sperm is needed to make a baby. Sperm are made in the male parts called "testicles." When a boy's body grows up, his two testicles will make an amazing amount of sperm—about one hundred million to three hundred million each day.

A female's egg is needed to make a baby. Eggs are stored inside the female parts called "ovaries." When a baby girl is born, her two ovaries have all the eggs—about one million to two million—she will ever need to make a baby.

Although boys are born with the parts that will make millions of sperm, and girls are born with the parts that store millions of eggs, those parts cannot make a baby until a child's body has grown up. And that time is called "puberty."

GROWING UP

Babies, Kids, Teenagers, Grown-ups

You've been growing up since you were a tiny baby. But puberty is the time when a girl's body changes and becomes a woman's body—and when a boy's body changes and becomes a man's body.

You may have even noticed kids who are going through puberty. Perhaps you have noticed an older brother or sister or cousin— or an older kid in your neighborhood or school—whose body is beginning to change and look more and more like an adult's body.

During puberty, girls' and boys' bodies change in many ways. These changes do not happen all at once. For most kids, these changes take place over a few years' time.

Since it takes a sperm and an egg to make a baby, a male and a female can *only* make a baby after puberty has begun. But most of the time, it's easier and healthier for people to wait to have a baby until they are older and have become grown-ups. That's because every baby needs a lot of love and care.

PEW-burr-tee? I have noticed THAT!

Yes. PU-ber-ty. I have not noticed a thing about it—NOT YET!

WHAT HAPPENS DURING PUBERTY?

- Boys and girls gain weight and grow taller.
- Girls and boys grow hair under their arms, on their arms, and on their legs.
- Boys and girls sweat more.
- Some girls and some boys get pimples on their faces, chests, and backs.
- Boys' voices become deeper.

- Girls' hips grow wider, and their breasts grow larger.
- Girls grow hair around the vulva—the area of soft skin between a female's legs.
- Boys grow hair on their upper lips and chests, and at the base of the penis.
- Girls' ovaries start to send out eggs.
- Boys' testicles start to make sperm.

So first you're a baby, then you're a kid, then you're a teenager, and then you're a grown-up. That's a lot of growing up to do!

I like being a kid. I'd like to stay being a kid. Wouldn't you?

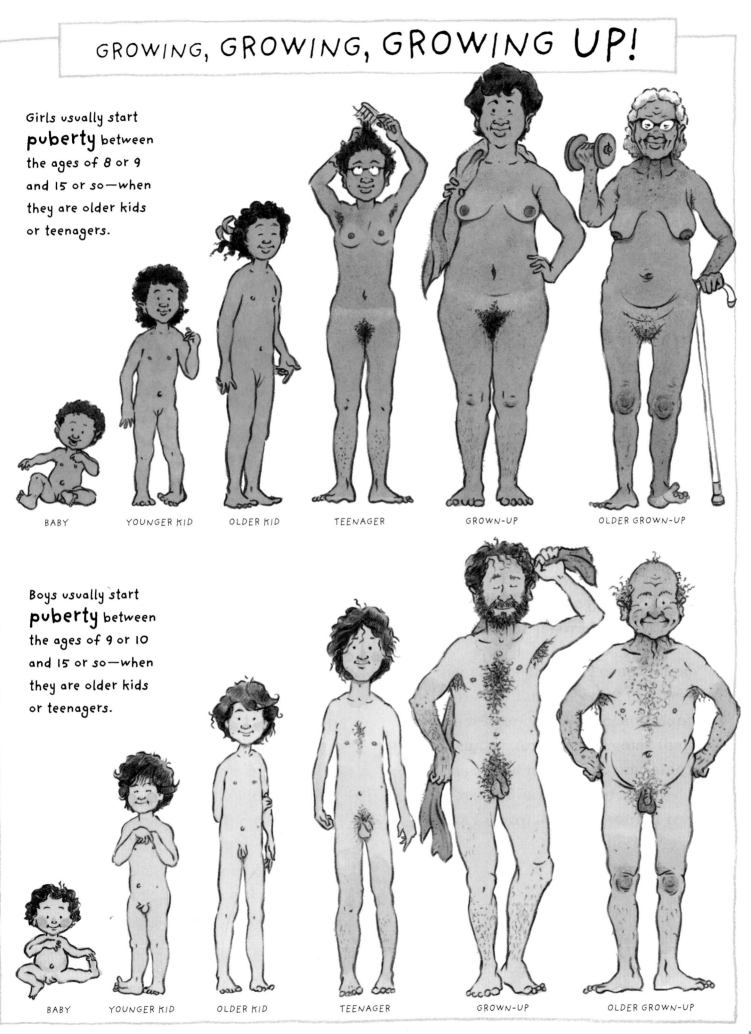

GROWING, GROWING, GROWING UP!

Girls usually start **puberty** between the ages of 8 or 9 and 15 or so—when they are older kids or teenagers.

BABY YOUNGER KID OLDER KID TEENAGER GROWN-UP OLDER GROWN-UP

Boys usually start **puberty** between the ages of 9 or 10 and 15 or so—when they are older kids or teenagers.

BABY YOUNGER KID OLDER KID TEENAGER GROWN-UP OLDER GROWN-UP

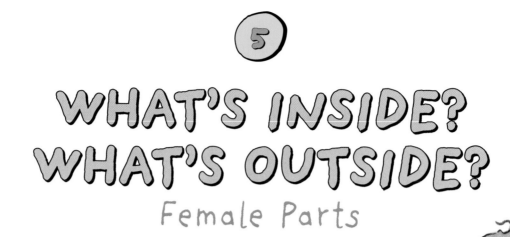

5

WHAT'S INSIDE? WHAT'S OUTSIDE?

Female Parts

Girls' bodies—even baby girls' bodies—and women's bodies have female parts. They are the parts that can make a baby—but *not* until *after* puberty has begun.

The female parts that are INSIDE baby girls', girls', and women's bodies are below the bellybutton and under the stomach and intestines.

Most of the female parts on the OUTSIDE of baby girls', girls', and women's bodies are tucked between a female's legs.

A female's breasts are also on the OUTSIDE of her body. They grow larger *after* puberty has begun. And if and when a female has a baby, her breasts can make milk to feed the baby.

Ohhh! So-ooo, female parts are—outside AND inside!

I don't care where they are—outside or inside—as long as we stop talking and talking about them!

WHAT'S INSIDE?

The two OVARIES hold a female's eggs. The ovaries are about the size of grapes or marbles when a girl is young. During puberty, a girl's two ovaries grow to be about the size of large strawberries.

OVARIES

The FALLOPIAN TUBES are two narrow tubes whose flowerlike openings are next to the ovaries. Each tube is about as wide as a soda straw. Each tube is connected to the uterus.

FALLOPIAN TUBES

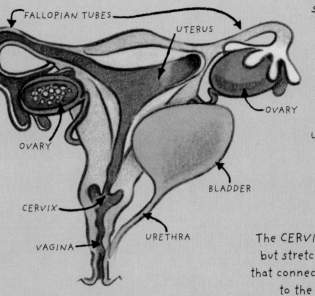

FALLOPIAN TUBES — UTERUS — OVARY — OVARY — CERVIX — VAGINA — URETHRA — BLADDER

The VAGINA is a small but stretchy passageway that leads from the uterus to a small opening between a female's legs.

The UTERUS is made of strong and stretchy muscles. It is about the size and shape of a small upside-down pear.

UTERUS

The CERVIX is a small but stretchy opening that connects the uterus to the vagina.

The URETHRA is a narrow tube that leads from the bladder to another small opening between a female's legs. Both females and males have a urethra and a bladder.

WHAT'S OUTSIDE?

The area of soft skin between a female's legs is called the VULVA.

Inside the vulva are two folds of soft skin called the LABIA. The labia cover and protect the inner parts of the vulva.

The CLITORIS—a small bump of skin about the size of a pea— is at the front of the labia.

Two openings—THE OPENING TO THE URETHRA and THE OPENING TO THE VAGINA— are tucked inside the labia.

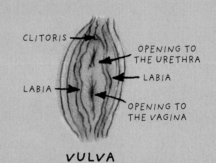

CLITORIS — OPENING TO THE URETHRA — LABIA — LABIA — OPENING TO THE VAGINA

VULVA

THE OPENING TO THE URETHRA is behind the clitoris. Urine—also called "pee"—leaves a female's body through the small opening to the urethra.

THE OPENING TO THE VAGINA is behind the opening to the urethra. When most babies are born, the baby comes out through the opening to the vagina.

Behind the labia is another small opening called the ANUS. Solid waste—also called "b.m." or "poop"—leaves a female's body through the anus. Both females *and* males have an anus.

In all, from front to back, there are three openings between a female's legs—the opening to her urethra, the opening to her vagina, and her anus.

6

WHAT'S INSIDE?
WHAT'S OUTSIDE?
Male Parts

Boys' bodies—even baby boys' bodies—and men's bodies
have male parts. They are the parts that can make
a baby—but *not* until *after* puberty has begun.

The male parts that are INSIDE baby boys', boys',
and men's bodies are below the bellybutton
and under the stomach and intestines.

The male parts on the OUTSIDE
of baby boys', boys', and men's bodies
hang between their legs.

I don't care if they are outside OR inside—OR inside out—as long as you stop TALKING about them!

And would you believe this? Male parts are outside AND inside too!

WHAT'S INSIDE?

The two TESTICLES make sperm after puberty has begun. The testicles are about the size of grapes or marbles when a boy is young. During puberty, a boy's two testicles grow to be the size of walnuts or very small balls. That's why some people call them "nuts" or "balls."

TESTICLES

The EPIDIDYMIS is a long, twisty, coiled tube. It is shaped somewhat like a pair of headphones, but smaller. Boys and men have two of these tubes. Each tube is connected to and wraps along the side of a testicle.

EPIDIDYMIS

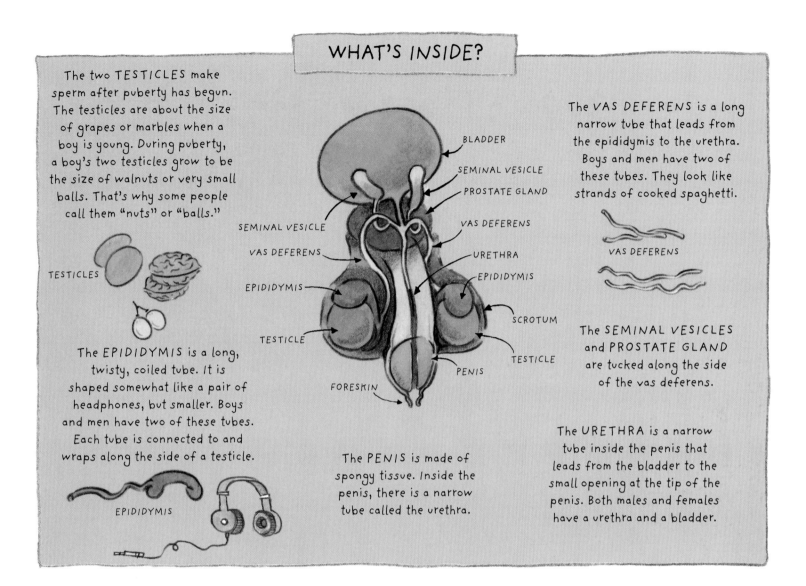

BLADDER

SEMINAL VESICLE

PROSTATE GLAND

SEMINAL VESICLE

VAS DEFERENS

VAS DEFERENS

URETHRA

EPIDIDYMIS

EPIDIDYMIS

SCROTUM

TESTICLE

TESTICLE

PENIS

FORESKIN

The PENIS is made of spongy tissue. Inside the penis, there is a narrow tube called the urethra.

The VAS DEFERENS is a long narrow tube that leads from the epididymis to the urethra. Boys and men have two of these tubes. They look like strands of cooked spaghetti.

VAS DEFERENS

The SEMINAL VESICLES and PROSTATE GLAND are tucked along the side of the vas deferens.

The URETHRA is a narrow tube inside the penis that leads from the bladder to the small opening at the tip of the penis. Both males and females have a urethra and a bladder.

WHAT'S OUTSIDE?

The PENIS hangs in front of the scrotum. There is a small opening at the tip of the penis.

The SCROTUM is a sac of soft, squishy skin that covers and protects the two testicles. After puberty has begun, the scrotum keeps the testicles at just the right temperature to make sperm.

The FORESKIN is a layer of loose skin that covers the end of the penis.

SCROTUM

FORESKIN

UNCIRCUMCISED PENIS

SCROTUM

CIRCUMCISED PENIS

Some male babies have the foreskin removed by a doctor or a specially trained religious person a few days after birth. This is called a "circumcision." Some male babies do not have the foreskin removed. Either way is perfectly normal.

Urine—also called "pee"—leaves a male's body through the small opening at the tip of the penis. After puberty has begun, sperm also leave through the tip of the penis. But urine and sperm do not leave the penis at the same time.

Behind the scrotum and penis is another small opening called the ANUS. Solid waste—also called "b.m." or "poop"—leaves a male's body through the anus. Both males and females have an anus.

In all, from front to back, there are two openings between a male's legs—the small opening at the tip of his penis, and his anus.

THE AMAZING EGG TRIP
What Do Eggs Do?

What eggs do is truly amazing! After girls begin puberty, about once a month a single egg pops out of an ovary and into one of the two narrow Fallopian tubes.

An egg that is ready to leave an ovary is about the size of a pencil dot.

When an egg meets and joins with a sperm . . .

. . . the united egg-and-sperm travels to the uterus where it can grow—over nine months' time—into a baby.

But most of the time, an egg does *not* meet a sperm. And if an egg does *not* meet a sperm, the beginning cells of a baby will *not* start to grow.

When an egg does *not* meet a sperm, the egg travels on to the uterus.

Then the egg breaks down and mixes with a small amount of blood from the uterus—and flows out of a girl's or woman's body through her vagina.

When the egg breaks down and leaves the uterus with the small amount of blood, this is called "menstruation," or "menstruating," or "having a period."

Men-stroo-a-shun?

Say a word 3 times and it's yours! Men-stru-a-tion! Men-struation! Menstruation!

The blood that flows out of the uterus and through the vagina does *not* come from a cut. And it does *not* appear because a girl or woman is sick or has been hurt. The blood comes from the soft lining of the uterus. And the lining and blood leave the uterus with the egg—and leave a girl's or woman's body through her vagina.

So that's what a "period" is.

The only period I know about is the one you make with a pencil. Period.

The blood from a period passes through the vagina and leaves a girl's or woman's body through the opening to her vagina. But urine, also called "pee," flows from the bladder—where it is stored—and flows through a passageway called the urethra. Urine leaves a girl's or woman's body through the opening to her urethra.

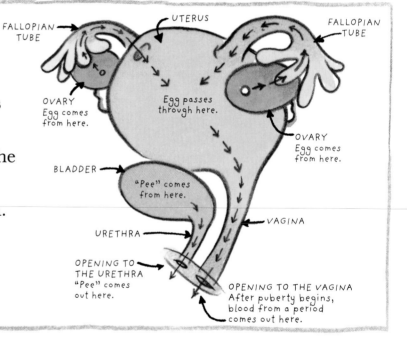

FALLOPIAN TUBE

UTERUS

FALLOPIAN TUBE

OVARY
Egg comes from here.

Egg passes through here.

BLADDER

"Pee" comes from here.

OVARY
Egg comes from here.

URETHRA

VAGINA

OPENING TO THE URETHRA
"Pee" comes out here.

OPENING TO THE VAGINA
After puberty begins, blood from a period comes out here.

Each new month, another egg is ready to leave one of the ovaries, and a new lining is made. The lining is needed only when a united egg-and-sperm cell—the beginning cells of a baby—starts to grow in the uterus.

I'M READY!

During a period, girls and women wear a soft, cottonlike "pad" inside their underpants, or a roll of cottonlike material that is shaped to fit inside the vagina. This is called a "tampon." The pad or tampon soaks up the small amount of blood so that it will not get on their clothes.

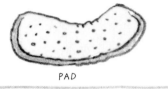

PAD   TAMPON

That's neat!

That's enough!

Girls do *not* begin to menstruate—to have periods—until *after* puberty has begun—sometime between the ages of eight or nine and fifteen or so. When a woman becomes pregnant, her periods stop. But they start again after her baby is born. At about age fifty, women stop having periods and do not have them again. That's because their ovaries stop sending out eggs.

Whew! I'm glad all that is PERFECTLY NORMAL.

Me too!

It's so amazing that if an egg meets a sperm, the beginning cells of a baby can start to grow! It's also amazing that if an egg does not meet a sperm, the egg travels out of the female's body— and the next month, another egg is ready to leave one of the ovaries!

Yep! This egg stuff is TRU-LY amazing.

The possibility of life on Mars . . . now that's what's REAL-LY amazing . . . to me.

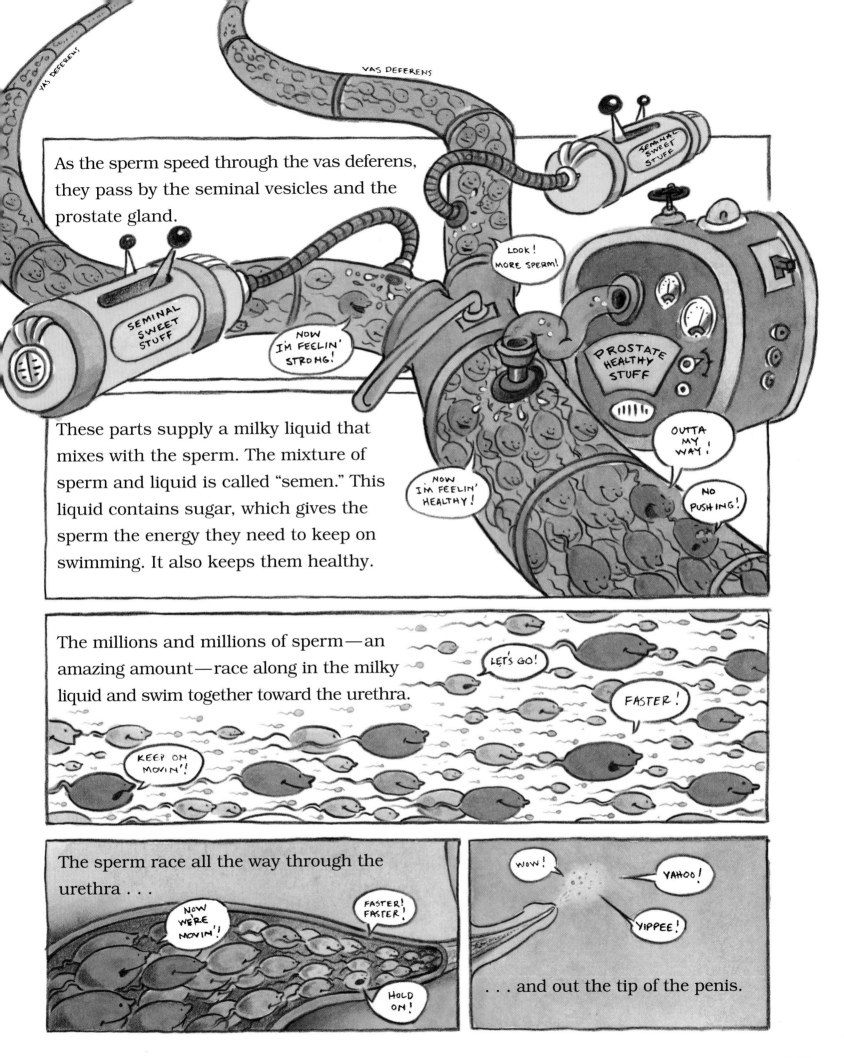

As the sperm speed through the vas deferens, they pass by the seminal vesicles and the prostate gland.

These parts supply a milky liquid that mixes with the sperm. The mixture of sperm and liquid is called "semen." This liquid contains sugar, which gives the sperm the energy they need to keep on swimming. It also keeps them healthy.

The millions and millions of sperm—an amazing amount—race along in the milky liquid and swim together toward the urethra.

The sperm race all the way through the urethra . . .

. . . and out the tip of the penis.

Sometimes the penis becomes stiff and larger, and stands out from the body. This is called "having an erection." After puberty begins, semen can—but does not always—come out the tip of the penis during an erection. When this happens, it is called an "ejaculation." And this is how sperm leave the penis.

A boy's testicles do *not* make sperm until *after* puberty begins. That's why sperm do *not* come out the tip of a young boy's penis. But older boys' and men's testicles *do* make sperm and continue to make sperm into old age.

And if just one of those sperm traveling along in the semen meets an egg, the beginning cells of a baby can start to grow.

Having an erection is perfectly healthy and perfectly normal at any age. Baby boys, boys, teenage boys, men, and old men have erections. Even before boy babies are born, they have erections inside the uterus.

Sometimes when a boy who has begun puberty—or a teenage boy or a man—has a dream, he may have an erection, and semen may come out the tip of his penis. This is called "having a wet dream." Boys do *not* begin to have wet dreams until *after* puberty begins—sometime between the ages of nine or ten and fifteen or so.

Whew! I'm glad all that is PERFECTLY NORMAL.

Me too!

Urine, also called "pee," flows from the bladder—where it is stored—and out boys' and men's bodies through the urethra and out the tip of the penis. But urine *does not* and *cannot* leave the penis at the same time as semen. That's because during an ejaculation, muscles at the top of the penis tighten and stop the urine from leaving.

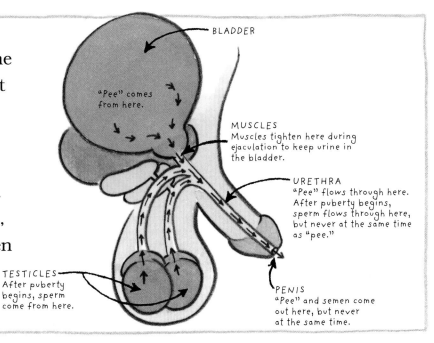

BLADDER

"Pee" comes from here.

MUSCLES
Muscles tighten here during ejaculation to keep urine in the bladder.

URETHRA
"Pee" flows through here. After puberty begins, sperm flows through here, but never at the same time as "pee."

TESTICLES
After puberty begins, sperm come from here.

PENIS
"Pee" and semen come out here, but never at the same time.

It's so amazing that if a sperm meets an egg, the beginning cells of a baby can start to grow! It's also amazing that millions of new sperm are made every day, and that sperm can swim so fast and so far!

Yep! This sperm stuff is TRU-LY amazing!

The fact that humans have walked on the moon... now that's what's REAL-LY amazing... to me.

WHAT'S SEX?

Male—Female—Loving—Making Love—Making a Baby

There's a good chance you know that making a baby has something to do with sex.

> I do know SOMETHING about making a baby . . .

> No comment . . .

But you may not know exactly what sex is.

> Well . . . I don't know EX-ACTLY what s-e-x is . . .

> No comment . . .

And you may wonder just what sex has to do with eggs and sperm.

> Well, I DO wonder about that!

> No comment . . .

Sex is how an egg and sperm can get together. But the word "sex"— like many words—means more than one thing.

> HUH?

> No comment . . .

If you have looked at your birth certificate, you may have noticed that the word "sex" is printed on it. And you may have noticed that the word "female" or "male," or the letter "F" or "M," is typed or written next to the word "sex."

> Oh look! It says s-e-x right there—right on my birth certificate!

> On mine, too!

Your birth certificate is a record of the day, the year, and the time of your birth. It's also a record of the city or town and the country you were born in, and of your weight and length on the day you were born. And it's also a record of whether you were born a member of the female sex or a member of the male sex.

But that's not all s-e-x means!

I can s-p-e-l-l, you know!

Whatever sex you were when you were born—female or male— is also called your "gender." Gender is also another word for all the thoughts and feelings a person may have about being male or female. Some people who are born female may feel or may know that they are male. And some who are born male may feel or may know that they are female. People who feel this way are called "transgender."

A girl?

It's a boy!

A boy?

So what sex is it?

It's a baby!

?!

Sex can be about other things, too—like loving, caring, and touching. Sex can also be about making a baby. When a woman and a man want to make a baby, they hug and cuddle and kiss and feel very loving, and get very close to each other—so close that the man's penis goes inside the woman's vagina. When this happens, it is called "sexual intercourse."

During sexual intercourse, millions of tiny sperm swim from the man's penis into the woman's vagina. And if just one of those sperm meets and joins together with an egg in one of the Fallopian tubes, the beginning cells of a baby can start to grow.

Some people call sexual intercourse "sex" or "having sex." When people grow up, having sex is one way to show their love for each other. That's why some people call sexual intercourse "making love." Grown-ups also make love when they are not planning to make a baby because it can feel good to be so close to each other.

Sexual intercourse may seem gross or nice, scary or funny, weird or cool—or even unbelievable to you. But when two people care for each other, sexual intercourse is very loving. Kids are much too young to have sexual intercourse.

Loving and taking good care of a baby and a child take a lot of time and work. That's why it makes good sense for people to wait to have a baby until they have had time to grow up and are ready to become parents.

10

WHAT'S LOVE?
Lots of Kinds of Love

When you like someone a whole lot and have warm and good and loving feelings about that person—that's called "love." There are times when love and sex go together. But love and sex do not always go together. Sometimes people just love each other.

My family's CRA-ZY about me! That's love!

My family BUZZES about me. That's love too!

Chances are you love many people—your parent, sister or brother, cousin, aunt or uncle, grandparent, or a family friend, or a good friend. And many people love you too.

I know another kind of love. I love playing the bass!

And I love playing the saxophone!

You may have a best friend—or a group of friends—whom you love to be with and who love to be with you. If you have a pet—a cat or a dog or a fish or a turtle or a guinea pig—you may also love your pet. You may also love a favorite stuffed animal. These kinds of love are not the same as "making love."

There are lots of kinds of love—like love between a parent and child, love between friends, love between kids, love between teenagers, and love between grown-ups. There can be love between a female and a male, or a male and a male, or a female and a female.

Isn't love just for—"lovebirds"?

Nope! Don't think so!

You may have heard the words "straight," "gay," and "lesbian." You may know—or you may wonder—what these words mean or what they have to do with love. You may have also heard the words "heterosexual" or "homosexual" or "bisexual." Although these three words have the word "sex" in them, they can also be about love.

More new words . . .

One thing I love is learning new words!

Here's what the words "straight," "gay," "lesbian," "heterosexual," "homosexual," and "bisexual" mean.

A female and a male who are sexually attracted to and who may fall in love with each other are called "straight." "Heterosexual" is another name for "straight." A person who is straight is someone who is sexually attracted— like a magnet—to the *other* sex or gender.

A male who is sexually attracted to another male and who may fall in love with another male is called "gay." "Homosexual" is another word for "gay." A female who is sexually attracted to another female and who may fall in love with another female is called "lesbian." "Gay" is another word for "lesbian." And so is "homosexual." A person who is gay or lesbian is someone who is sexually attracted—like a magnet—to a person of the *same* sex or gender.

A person who is bisexual is someone who is sexually attracted—like a magnet—to people of the *other* sex or gender and also to people of the *same* sex or gender.

A person's daily life—having friends, having fun, going to work, being a parent, loving another person—is mostly the same no matter who you are or who you love.

There are lots of wonderful ways that people of all ages show their love for another person. Hugging, cuddling, holding hands, or giving someone a kiss are all wonderful ways to show love. So is spending time with someone, or telling someone "I love you!"

I LOVE YOU!

Wait a minute! I thought we were talking sperm and egg and baby stuff here.

E-nough about all that stuff! E-nough about lovey-dovey stuff too!

THE BIG RACE!

Sperm and Egg Meet

It takes only one egg and one sperm to make a baby.

When a man and a woman have sexual intercourse, millions of tiny sperm traveling along in the semen race out the tip of the man's penis and quickly swim into the woman's vagina.

Sperm are shaped like tadpoles. Their long tails are what make them such speedy swimmers. When scientists watch sperm swim under a microscope, they can actually see the sperm's tails whipping and lashing back and forth.

After the sperm swim through the vagina, they race through a narrow opening called the cervix, and into the uterus.

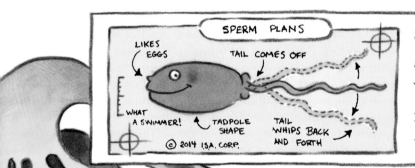

Then the sperm swim through the uterus and into the two narrow Fallopian tubes. If an egg has left an ovary and is in one of the Fallopian tubes, that's where a sperm can meet an egg.

It usually takes several hours for the millions of sperm to swim all the way to the Fallopian tubes.

Usually only about two hundred sperm— out of the millions of sperm—swim to and get close to an egg.

Scientists have discovered that if an egg is in one of the tubes, a chemical in the liquid around the egg attracts one sperm out of the two hundred sperm—just like a magnet.

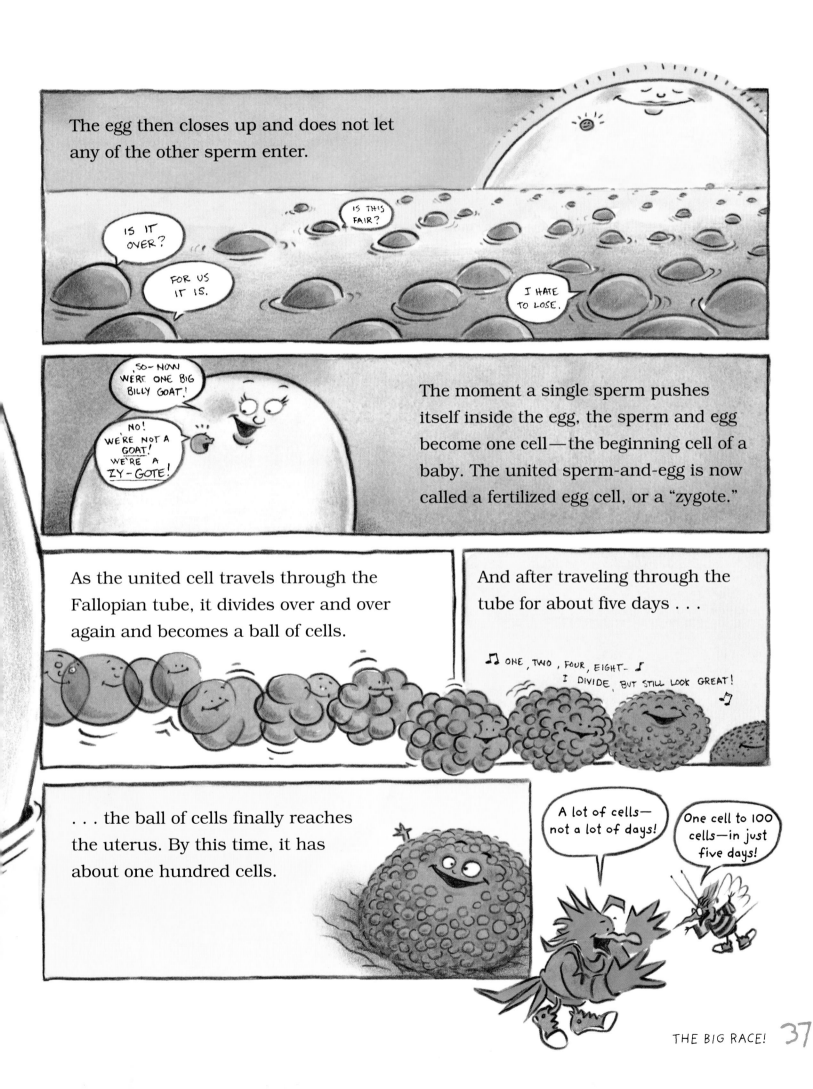

The egg then closes up and does not let any of the other sperm enter.

IS IT OVER?

IS THIS FAIR?

FOR US IT IS.

I HATE TO LOSE.

SO— NOW WE'RE ONE BIG BILLY GOAT!

NO! WE'RE NOT A GOAT! WE'RE A ZY-GOTE!

The moment a single sperm pushes itself inside the egg, the sperm and egg become one cell—the beginning cell of a baby. The united sperm-and-egg is now called a fertilized egg cell, or a "zygote."

As the united cell travels through the Fallopian tube, it divides over and over again and becomes a ball of cells.

And after traveling through the tube for about five days . . .

ONE, TWO, FOUR, EIGHT— I DIVIDE, BUT STILL LOOK GREAT!

. . . the ball of cells finally reaches the uterus. By this time, it has about one hundred cells.

A lot of cells— not a lot of days!

One cell to 100 cells—in just five days!

Sometimes when people want to have a baby, the egg cell and sperm cell are not able to meet. That's when some people choose to adopt a baby or child. And that's when some people use ways other than sexual intercourse for an egg cell and a sperm cell to meet. In fact, scientists have figured out several ways for an egg cell and a sperm cell to meet.

So the sperm and egg meet at the swim meet!

They don't meet at the track meet!

Doctors can place sperm into the vagina or the uterus with a syringe—a tube like an eyedropper.

YIPPEE!

YAHOO!

The sperm can then swim to the Fallopian tubes, where a sperm can meet and join with an egg . . .

HI!

LET'S JOIN TOGETHER!

. . . and travel to the uterus, where the beginning cells of a baby can start to grow.

THIS IS JUST THE BEGINNING!

Or doctors can put an egg and a sperm in a special laboratory dish where the egg and sperm can meet and join together.

HI! *HI!*

After they have joined, the doctor uses a syringe to place the united egg-and-sperm cell into the uterus . . .

WHOOPEE!

. . . where the beginning cells of a baby can start to grow.

I'M GOING, GOING, GOING, I'm GOING TO KEEP ON GROWING!

That's awesome science!

Right on! Science IS awesome!

There are times when a man and a woman have sexual intercourse, but do not wish to make a baby. Scientists have invented ways called "birth control" that can keep a sperm and egg from meeting. And if a sperm and egg do not meet, the beginning cells of a baby cannot start to grow.

There are many kinds of birth control. One kind is a "condom." A condom can catch sperm before it can meet the egg. A condom fits over the penis. A condom can also keep people from getting or passing on infections like HIV—the infection that causes AIDS—during sexual intercourse. Another kind of birth control is a pill a woman can take. These pills can keep the ovaries from sending out an egg.

The only sure way for people *not* to have a baby or *not* to get an infection from sex is *not* to have sexual intercourse. And that is called "abstinence." Abstinence and birth control can help people choose whether or not to have a baby— or how many children to have— or when to have a baby.

A WARM AND COZY WOMB

Pregnancy

It's so amazing that a tiny ball of cells can grow into a whole new person—a baby! But it can. Once the ball of cells arrives inside the uterus, it plants itself in the soft lining of the uterus.

It's so amazing that over nine months' time those cells will divide billions and billions of times to grow and become a baby! It takes a lot of time and growing to become a baby.

A woman is "pregnant" once the ball of cells starts to grow in the lining of her uterus. Now the ball of cells is called an "embryo." By three months, an embryo is called a "fetus." It is called a fetus until it is ready to be born.

As a fetus grows bigger, the uterus gets bigger and stretches wide—like a balloon—to make more room. When a woman is pregnant, her uterus stretches from the size of a small pear to about the size of a watermelon. After eight or nine months of growing, the fetus moves around less because there's less room inside the uterus. After the baby is born, its mother's uterus shrinks back to its regular shape and size.

PITH·H·H·H·S·SSSSS······

"Pregnancy" is the time it takes for an embryo to become a fetus and for a fetus to be born. Then it's a baby! A lot of kids—and even some grown-ups—think that a fetus grows in its mother's stomach. A fetus does not grow in the stomach. A fetus grows in the uterus. Some people call the fetus "a growing baby."

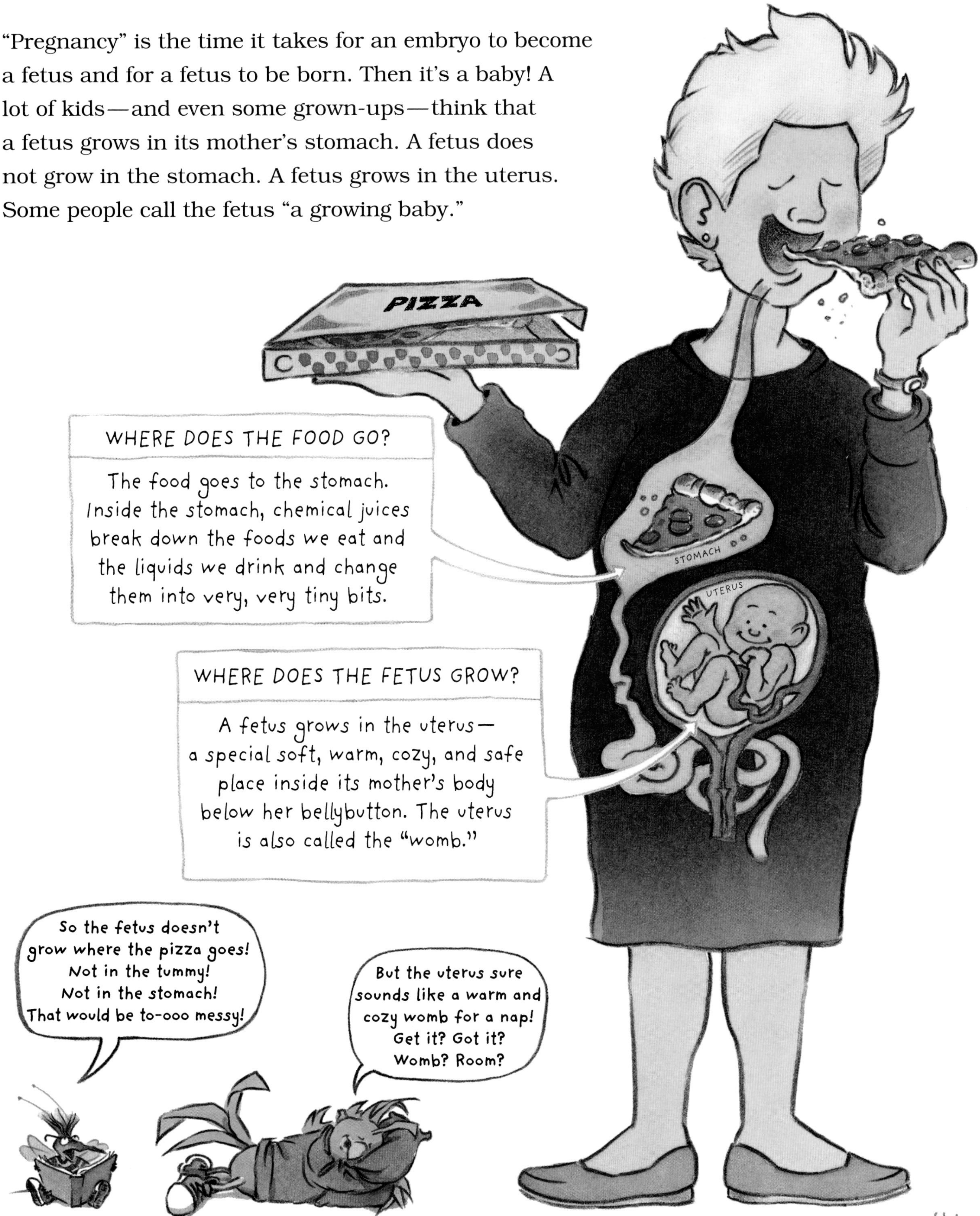

PIZZA

WHERE DOES THE FOOD GO?

The food goes to the stomach. Inside the stomach, chemical juices break down the foods we eat and the liquids we drink and change them into very, very tiny bits.

STOMACH

UTERUS

WHERE DOES THE FETUS GROW?

A fetus grows in the uterus— a special soft, warm, cozy, and safe place inside its mother's body below her bellybutton. The uterus is also called the "womb."

So the fetus doesn't grow where the pizza goes! Not in the tummy! Not in the stomach! That would be to-ooo messy!

But the uterus sure sounds like a warm and cozy womb for a nap! Get it? Got it? Womb? Room?

There are times when a pregnancy ends without warning—before an embryo or fetus is big enough and healthy enough to live outside the uterus. When this happens, it is called a "miscarriage." Most women who have had a miscarriage can become pregnant again and give birth to a strong and healthy baby.

And there are times when a woman becomes pregnant and then chooses not to stay pregnant. She may then choose to have an "abortion." An abortion is a medical way to end a pregnancy. Most women who have had an abortion can become pregnant again and give birth to a strong and healthy baby.

And there are times when a woman who is pregnant chooses not to bring up her baby. She may choose to stay pregnant and make a plan for her baby to be adopted. And when her baby is born, the baby can be adopted by a family who can love, care for, and bring up that baby.

HOW LONG UNTIL IT'S A BABY?
Pregnancy

BALL OF CELLS TO BABY
9 Months of Growing

A pregnancy begins when the **BALL OF CELLS** plants itself in the lining of the uterus and becomes an embryo. By now, it has about 100 cells and is about the size of a pin point.

By **1 MONTH,** an embryo is about the size of a tomato seed. Its backbone has begun to grow and its heart has begun to beat.

By **1½ MONTHS,** an embryo is about the size of a blueberry. The very beginnings of its arms, legs, fingers, toes, ears, eyes, nose, and lips have begun to form.

By **2 MONTHS,** an embryo is about the size of a peach pit. By now, its fingers, toes, ears, eyes, nose, and lips show. And its eyelids have begun to form.

By **3 MONTHS,** when an embryo has become a fetus, it is about the size of a large peach. The parts that make a fetus male or female have formed. Fingernails and toenails have begun to grow. A fetus's body begins to be covered by soft fuzzy hair called "lanugo," and a slippery whitish coating called "vernix." The hair and coating protect a fetus from the water it floats in.

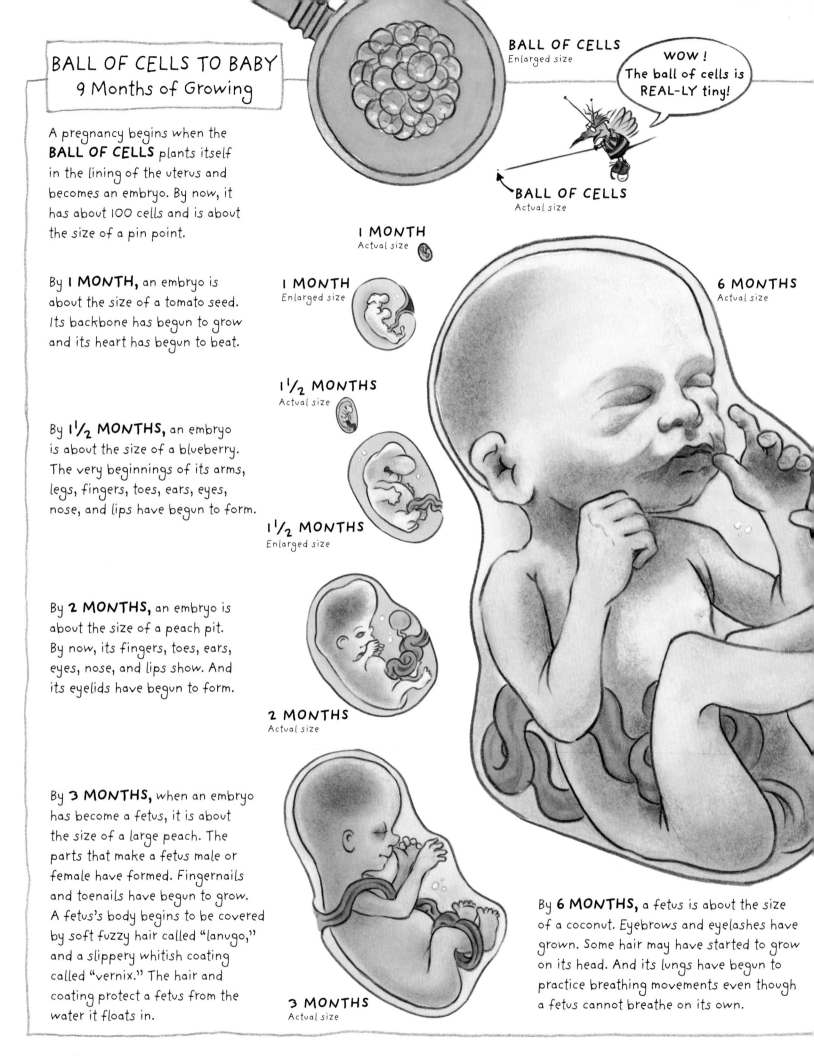

BALL OF CELLS
Enlarged size

WOW!
The ball of cells is REAL-LY tiny!

BALL OF CELLS
Actual size

1 MONTH
Actual size

1 MONTH
Enlarged size

1½ MONTHS
Actual size

1½ MONTHS
Enlarged size

2 MONTHS
Actual size

3 MONTHS
Actual size

6 MONTHS
Actual size

By **6 MONTHS,** a fetus is about the size of a coconut. Eyebrows and eyelashes have grown. Some hair may have started to grow on its head. And its lungs have begun to practice breathing movements even though a fetus cannot breathe on its own.

By **9 MONTHS,** most fetuses—but not all—are facing head down. And by now, a fetus has grown bigger, longer, and fatter and has millions and millions and millions of cells. Its brain, heart, lungs, stomach, and other parts of its body are all working well. It is about the size of a water-melon—weighing about five to eleven pounds. It's ready to be born—to be a baby!

9 MONTHS
Actual size

It's SO-OOO A-MAZING that this drawing is life-size!

FRESH FOOD! FRESH AIR!

Growing and Staying Healthy

Inside the uterus, a sac filled with warm water surrounds the embryo—and then the fetus—and keeps it warm and safe as it grows. The sac is called the "amniotic sac." The fetus floats in the warm water. The warm water is called "amniotic fluid." The sac and the water protect the fetus from pokes and jolts and bumps.

Every so often, the fetus drinks some of the warm water it floats in. The water inside the uterus is perfectly healthy for a fetus to drink.

While the fetus is inside the uterus, it needs food and air, just like we all do—to grow and stay healthy. But a fetus cannot eat food the way we do or breathe air on its own.

46   IT'S SO AMAZING!

WARM AND SAFE IN THE UTERUS

The healthy foods and liquids a pregnant woman eats and drinks supply the fetus with the good things it needs to grow and stay healthy. And the air she breathes supplies the fetus with the oxygen it needs.

The food and air the fetus needs travel to a soft spongy place inside the mother's uterus called the "placenta."

The fetus is connected to the placenta by a thick twisty cord called the "umbilical cord." Your bellybutton—also called your "navel"—is the place where the umbilical cord was attached to you when you were growing inside the uterus.

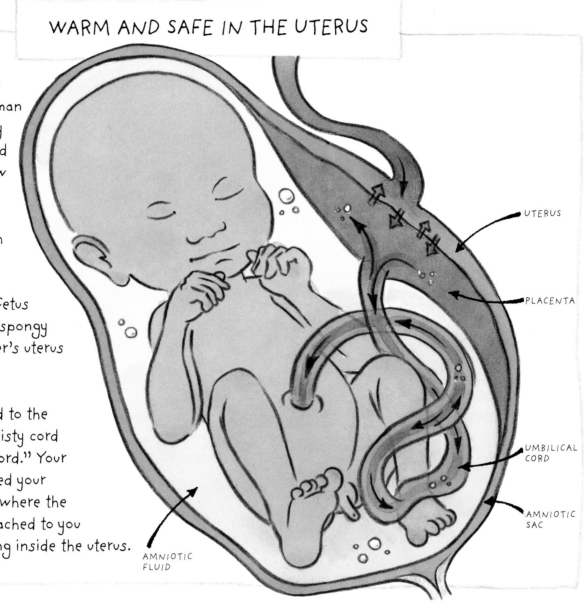

UTERUS

PLACENTA

UMBILICAL CORD

AMNIOTIC SAC

AMNIOTIC FLUID

The bits of food and air the fetus does not need leave through the umbilical cord. Some bits of the food and air also leave the fetus's body in the small amount of urine—also called "pee"—it makes. The fetus's "pee" becomes part of the water in the uterus. Usually a fetus does not "poop" while it's in the uterus.

Sometimes unhealthy things can pass into a pregnant woman's blood and into the fetus—cigarette smoke, and many kinds of drugs, including alcohol from wine, beer, or liquor. Most pregnant women are very careful about what they eat and drink, and what medicines they take. They want to do everything possible to give birth to a healthy baby.

STRETCH! PUNCH! KICK! HICCUP! BURP!
The Growing Fetus

While a fetus is growing inside the uterus, it does a lot of things! It can make a fist and punch. It can kick its feet. It can even do somersaults. It can suck its thumb and fingers. And it can taste, swallow, and blink and open its eyes. It can also stretch and sleep. And it can make noises—like hiccups and burps!

A fetus can also hear. It can hear the sound of its mother's voice, the sound of her stomach rumbling, the sound of her heart beating, and of her blood pumping through her body.

It can hear noises like a doorbell ringing, or a piano being played, or a song being sung. You could do all of these things, too—when you were growing inside the uterus.

After a woman is about four or five months pregnant, at times she can feel the fetus moving. When a fetus hears a loud sound, or when a bright light or bright sunshine shines on the uterus, a fetus may move suddenly. A pregnant woman can feel when a fetus is moving a lot and when it is quiet and resting.

You might like to ask a woman who is pregnant—your mother or an aunt or a family friend or a friend's mother—if you can put your hand on her belly. When a fetus has grown big enough, you may be able to see and feel the fetus move and stretch its arms and legs, or punch its fist, or kick its feet.

You may also be able to see the shape of the fetus's body, or elbow, or knee, or fist, or foot. And when the fetus moves, sometimes you can see that, too. Moving and stretching and kicking and punching don't hurt the mother at all—but she can feel it.

> I'd tell it, "It's the middle of the night! Go back to sleep!"

> I'd talk to the fetus or sing it a lullaby!

> I bet a kick or punch can even wake her up at night . . .

> . . . or at the movies—if she's snoozing.

Sometimes the doctor or nurse will take a moving computer picture of the fetus while it is inside the uterus. This type of picture is taken to make sure that the fetus is growing well and is healthy. It is taken by a special computer and is called an "ultrasound."

If you watch the computer screen, you might see the fetus move its hands and legs, or blink, or suck its thumb, or move around, or even turn over. You might be able to see its heart beating. You might even see if the fetus has a penis or a vagina.

You might be able to see if one fetus or two—twins—or more are growing inside the uterus. Your family may have a photograph of an ultrasound of you—or your sister, or brother, or cousin.

I love to look at pictures of me!

I'm sure you do-ooo! . . .

STRETCH! PUNCH! KICK! HICCUP! BURP! 53

⑮ TWINS AND MORE!

Twins, Triplets, Quadruplets, Quintuplets

Most of the time when a sperm and egg meet, the beginning cells of only one baby start to grow. But another amazing thing can happen the moment an egg and sperm meet. Although it does not happen often, the beginning cells of two babies—twins—can start to grow.

TWINS! More totally amazing things!

E-nough totally amazing things! E-nough!

HOW DO TWINS BEGIN?

Identical Twins

If an egg that has been fertilized by a sperm splits into two while it is in the Fallopian tube, the beginning cells of two babies— identical twins—can start to grow in the uterus.

1 egg   +   1 sperm   join and split in 2   =   the beginning cells of identical twins

Fraternal Twins

Twins can also begin if two eggs happen to be in the Fallopian tube. If those two eggs join with two sperm, the beginning cells of two babies—fraternal twins—can start to grow in the uterus.

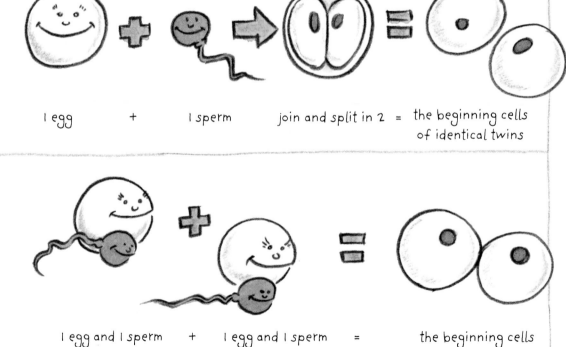

1 egg and 1 sperm   +   1 egg and 1 sperm   =   the beginning cells of fraternal twins

Identical Twins

Identical means "the same." Identical twins look almost exactly alike and are always the same sex. When identical twins are born, they are always either two girls or two boys.

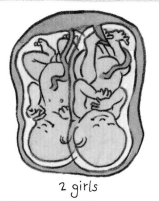

2 girls   or   2 boys

Fraternal Twins

Fraternal twins do not look exactly alike. When fraternal twins are born, they are either a boy and a girl, two boys, or two girls.

A boy and a girl   or   2 boys   or   2 girls

Triplets

If three eggs and three sperm join together in the Fallopian tube, or if a fertilized egg splits into three, the beginning cells of three babies—triplets—can start to grow in the uterus.

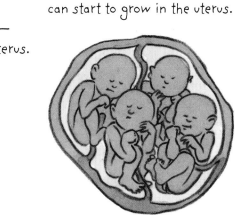

Quadruplets

Sometimes, the beginning cells of four babies—quadruplets—can start to grow in the uterus.

Quintuplets

Sometimes, the beginning cells of five babies—quintuplets—can start to grow in the uterus.

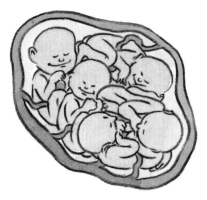

Triplets, quadruplets, and quintuplets—like twins—can be identical or fraternal. Or they can be a mixture of both.

TRI means "three," QUAD means "four," and QUIN means "five"—in Latin. What I bet you can say is "TRIP-lets." But can you say "QUAD-rup-lets"? or "QUIN-tup-lets"?

All I'd say is—that's a whole lot of babies! "Kwad-RUPE-lets"? "Kwin-TUP-lets"? Hey, hey, hey! "Kwin" rhymes with "twin"!

COME OUT, COME OUT, WHEREVER YOU ARE!

Birth

After nine months inside the uterus, the fetus has grown big enough and strong enough and is ready to be born. Being born can take a long time—sometimes more than a day. Or it can take just a few hours.

How does the baby know when to come out?

Someone must shout, "Come out, come out, wherever you are!"

Most babies are born in hospitals. Some babies are born at home. People who are specially trained—a doctor or midwife, and nurses—help the mother while her baby is being born. Fathers, and sometimes other family members and friends, often help, too.

I was born in a tree!

I was born in the ground!

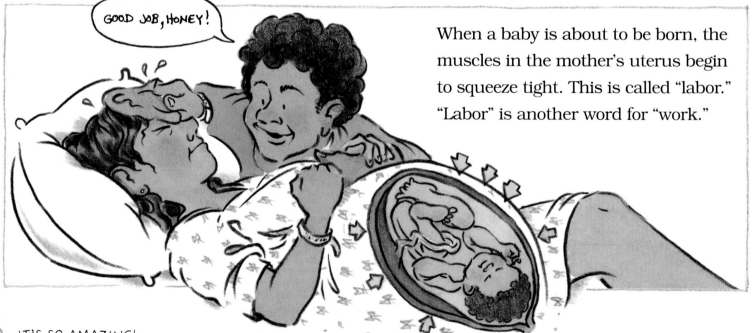

GOOD JOB, HONEY!

When a baby is about to be born, the muscles in the mother's uterus begin to squeeze tight. This is called "labor." "Labor" is another word for "work."

A mother's muscles work very hard to push and squeeze the baby out of the uterus and into the vagina. Then the mother's muscles push and squeeze the baby's body through the vagina.

The vagina stretches wide as the baby's soft, wet, and slippery body travels through it. It's a tight squeeze, but finally the baby slides out—and is born!

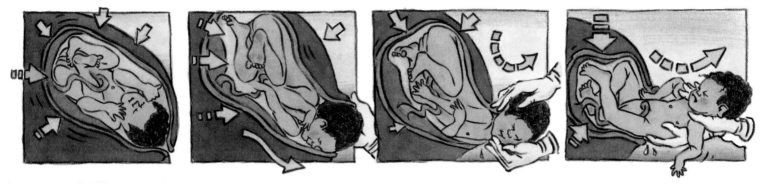

The moment of birth is so exciting! The doctor or midwife, or sometimes the baby's father, gently holds the baby as it comes out. That's when most babies let out their first cry. And that's when someone often shouts out, "It's a girl!" or "It's a boy!"—even if the parent or parents already knew the sex of the baby before birth.

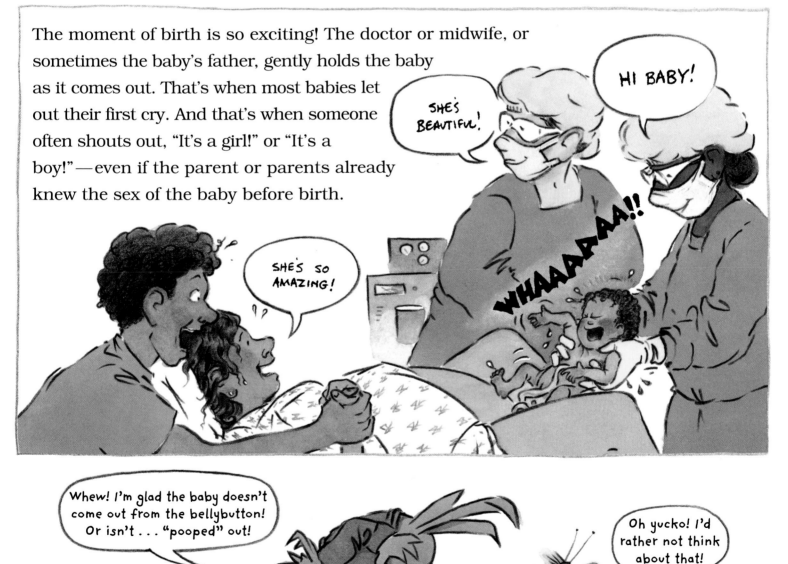

Whether it is soft or loud, a baby's first cry fills up its lungs with fresh air. This is how a baby takes its first breath and starts breathing on its own.

WHAAAH!

YOU DID IT!

Seconds later, the doctor—or sometimes a midwife or a close family member—cuts the cord. This is the cord that connected the baby to its mother and gave it food and air. The cord is cut because the mother no longer needs to eat and breathe for the baby. The cutting does not hurt the baby or the mother.

As soon as the cord is cut—or sometimes even before—the baby's parents are usually able to hold, cuddle, kiss, and hug their new baby. It feels so wonderful when a parent can finally hold and look at the new baby.

The tiny piece of cord that is left on the baby's body dries up and falls off—after a week or so. The place where the cord was attached becomes a person's navel. It often looks like a button, and that's probably why many people call the navel a "bellybutton."

Are you an "innie" or an "outie"?

Never checked, thank you.

A few minutes later, the placenta and amniotic sac pass out of the mother's body through her vagina. The placenta is no longer needed to help the baby eat and breathe. The sac is no longer needed to hold and protect the baby.

I can breathe and eat on my own.

Speaking of eating— I'm hungry!

PIZZA

Most babies are born head first. Some are born feet first. And most are born through the vagina. But if a baby is too big, or is in a difficult position in the uterus—like sideways—the doctor makes a cut through the mother's skin and into her uterus. The mother is given some medicine before the cut is made, so she won't feel pain. After the cut is made, the baby is lifted out—and is born!

Then the umbilical cord is cut. The placenta and amniotic sac are lifted out and the cut in the mother's skin and uterus is sewn with a special thread. This cut heals in a few weeks' time. When a baby is born this way, it is called a "cesarean birth" or a "c-section." A cesarean birth is another perfectly normal and healthy way to be born.

HELLO BABY!

WHAAAA!!

HE'S SO AMAZING!

HE'S BEAUTIFUL!

It says here: "The name 'cesarean' comes from the name of the great Roman leader Julius Caesar. Historians believe that Caesar may have been born this way in ancient Rome around 100 B.C.— more than 2,000 years ago." Now THAT is interesting!

If it was good enough for Caesar, it's good enough for me.

Some babies are born before they have spent a whole nine months in the uterus. Babies who are born early are called "premature" babies or "preemies." Preemies often have to stay in the hospital for some extra time until they learn to suck well. This helps them eat well. They also need to stay until they have gained enough weight to keep their bodies warm enough.

While they are in the hospital, preemies usually sleep in a special crib called an "incubator." The incubator keeps the baby warm and provides fresh air for the baby to breathe as it continues to grow.

A preemie's parent or parents spend lots of time in the hospital getting to know their baby. They can touch, hold, kiss, talk to, sing to, and feed their baby.

When the baby grows bigger and stronger, its parents or parent can take their baby home.

New babies need to be fed. Milk is the only food they need until they are older. After a baby is born, its mother's breasts begin to make milk. When a baby sucks and drinks milk from its mother's breasts, the mother's breasts make more milk. Breast milk contains all the vitamins, sugars, fats, salt, and other things a young baby needs to grow and stay healthy. Sometimes babies are fed breast milk from a bottle.

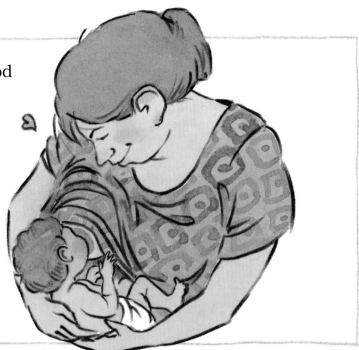

Some babies are fed formula from a bottle. Formula is different from breast milk. Formula is made from cow's milk or soy milk, which is made from the bean of the soybean plant. Vitamins, sugars, fats, salt, and other things are added to help a young baby grow and stay healthy. Babies suck and drink formula through a special nipple that's attached to a bottle.

When babies are several months old, they can start to eat other foods. And by their first birthday, most babies can drink cow's milk—just like most older kids and grown-ups do.

So let's celebrate and have a milk shake!

Being born is one of the MOST A-MAZING THINGS that EVER HAPPENS!

WHAT MAKES YOU—YOU!

Chromosomes and Genes—And Other Things, Too!

You may wonder how you happened to be born a boy or a girl, or with curly hair instead of straight hair. These things are decided the moment a sperm cell and an egg cell join together—long before a baby is born.

Back to egg and sperm again?

Yep! That's when what makes you YOU starts!

Inside every egg and sperm are chromosomes. Chromosomes look like tiny threads and are so small they can be seen only under a microscope. All sperm have an X or a Y chromosome. All eggs have an X chromosome.

If a sperm with a Y chromosome joins with an egg, a male baby—a boy—will be born. If a sperm with an X chromosome joins with an egg, a female baby—a girl—will be born. That means that females have two X chromosomes and males have one X chromosome and one Y chromosome.

Chrom-o-some. I like saying that word.

Why? X and Y are much easier to say—and to write.

Strung along our chromosomes—like beads on a necklace—are tiny, tiny parts called "genes." Genes contain thousands of pieces of information about a person—such as whether a person has brown or blue eyes, or small or large hands. Your genes were passed on to you from your parents when the sperm and the egg that made you joined together.

Genes? Beads? Necklace? I don't get it! I'm all mixed up!

You ARE all mixed up! 'Cause the genes from an egg—and the genes from a sperm—got all mixed up together—to make YOU!

The color of your eyes and hair and skin, the size of your feet, the shape of your ears, the shape of your body, how short or tall you are—and thousands of other things about you—were all passed on to you from your parents' genes. If you were adopted, your genes were passed on to you by the woman and man—called your "birth parents"—whose egg and sperm joined to make you.

But you are not an exact copy of either parent whose sperm and egg joined together to make you. That's because you received a mixture of genes from both of them, and from their parents and grandparents, and from their ancestors. That's why if you have a brother or sister, you can look somewhat different—or very different—from each other. That's why you may look a lot like your parents— or hardly at all like your parents.

Who you are is not decided by genes and chromosomes alone. All the people you grow up with, all the things you do, all that happens to you—along with all the genes that mixed together to make you—are what make you different from any other person. That's why no person in the world is exactly like you—even if you are an identical twin.

BECOMING A FAMILY
By Birth—By Adoption

Every family is different. Almost all babies and children grow up in families and are taken care of by their families. Babies and children grow up in all sorts of families.

> Small families, middle-size families . . .

> . . . and big families!

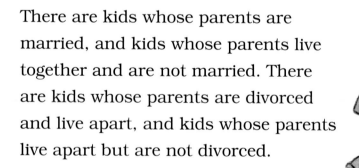

There are kids whose parents are married, and kids whose parents live together and are not married. There are kids whose parents are divorced and live apart, and kids whose parents live apart but are not divorced.

There are kids who grow up with their birth parents, and kids whose parent or parents have adopted them. There are kids who grow up with one parent. There are kids who live with one parent part of the time and with their other parent the rest of the time.

There are kids whose parent or parents are straight, or whose parent or parents are gay men or are lesbian women, or who are bisexual or transgender. There are kids who live with a parent and a stepparent, or who live with an aunt, an uncle, a grandmother, a grandfather, or other relatives. Sometimes kids live with a foster parent or parents while their own parent or parents or a social worker figures out who would be the best person to take loving and good care of them.

Hey! All kinds of families!

Hey! All kinds of kids!

Parents, grandparents, cousins, uncles, and aunts are all part of a person's family. And for many people, good friends are part of their families, too. Most kids are loved and taken care of by family members and family friends.

Most babies are born into their family. Some babies are adopted into their family. But the beginning cell of every baby starts when a woman's egg and a man's sperm join and become one cell. This united egg-and-sperm cell divides again and again and travels to the woman's uterus—where it grows until a baby is born. That woman and that man are your parents unless you were adopted.

If you were adopted, the woman whose egg helped to make you is called your "birth mother" or "biological mother." And the man whose sperm helped to make you is called your "birth father" or "biological father."

I have a very close family—"birds of a feather flock together."

I have a very busy family—"busy as bees!"

There are times when a birth mother or birth father or birth parents cannot take care of their baby or child. When this happens, they make a plan for their baby or child to be adopted—to become a member of another family and be cared for and loved by that family.

Some people choose to adopt because they are not able to give birth to a child. Other people who can give or have given birth to a baby also choose to adopt.

I like to be loved!

Don't we all!

When a parent or parents adopt a child, that means they will love and raise that baby or child as their child.

In the United States when a baby or child is adopted, most of the time the birth parent or birth parents sign a paper that says they have chosen to give their child to a parent or parents who want to and are able to take care of their child. And the new adopting parent or parents sign a paper and agree in front of a judge to care for, raise, and protect the child they have chosen to adopt.

Babies and children are also adopted from other countries around the world. When a baby or child is adopted from another country, that baby or child can become a citizen of the United States.

When a baby or child is adopted, its parent or parents often have a party or ceremony and invite family members to meet and celebrate their new baby or child. Choosing to adopt a baby or child is another way for a grown-up to become a parent and for a baby or child to be cared for and loved.

Adoption's an awesome thing!

It's an awesome way to make a family!

KEEPING SAFE
"Okay Touches"—"Not Okay Touches"

Every family's job is to love, take care of, and keep their babies and children safe. One very important thing to know about staying safe is that your body belongs to you.

The female parts of girls' and women's bodies and the male parts of boys' and men's bodies are often called "privates." The private parts of a person's body are the parts that are usually covered by underpants or by a bathing suit.

My body belongs to me.

My body is private.

When your parent takes you for a checkup, the reason your doctor or nurse has to look at or touch the private parts of your body is to make sure every part of your body is healthy.

If your privates ever feel uncomfortable or hurt, it's important to tell a parent— or another adult you know well and trust. Then that person can take you to your doctor or nurse for a checkup. Always tell your doctor or nurse if any part of your body hurts, or has been hurt, or feels uncomfortable.

It's perfectly normal to be curious about your own body—how it looks, feels, and works. It's also perfectly normal to want some private time for yourself and to have some privacy when you are getting dressed or taking a bath or a shower.

Touching or rubbing the private parts of your own body because it feels good is called "masturbation." Some people also call masturbation "playing with yourself." Many people masturbate. Many don't.

Every family has its own thoughts and feelings about masturbation. Your family may feel differently from your friend's or cousin's or neighbor's family about whether it's okay, or not okay, to masturbate. Some people and some religions think it's wrong to masturbate. But most doctors agree that masturbation is perfectly healthy and perfectly normal— and cannot hurt you or your body.

But if any person touches any part of your body and you do not want them to, say "STOP!" or "NO!" or "DON'T!" It is your right to say that—even if the person is someone in your family or someone you know—even if the person is bigger, older, or stronger than you are.

You may have heard the words "sexual abuse." Sexual abuse happens when someone touches the private parts of a person's body and does NOT have the right to do that.

STOP!

NO! NO! NO!

DON'T!

Sexual abuse is always wrong, and most adults know that it is wrong. Sexual abuse can hurt. Or it can feel gentle. This can be very confusing because it's almost impossible to understand how something so wrong can feel gentle.

It's hard to hear about this.

It's hard to talk about this.

If sexual abuse ever happens to you—it is NEVER your fault. And do NOT keep it a secret even if someone tells you to keep it a secret. There are some secrets that are okay to keep, but sexual abuse is not one of them. You must make sure that you tell another person right away—someone in your family, or your teacher, or doctor, or nurse, or school nurse, or clergy member, or someone you know very well and trust.

So there are "not okay touches" . . .

. . . not okay . . . EVER . . . AT ALL!

Most of the time, the person you tell will do all he or she can to keep the abuse from happening again. But if the first person you tell doesn't listen or believe you, tell a second person. Talk about it until you find someone who does listen and believes you. He or she will try to keep you safe and protect you from the person who tried to touch you or did touch you. Most adults *do* care about kids and want to keep them safe.

> I DO like hugs and kisses—every day.

> I do NOT like too-tight hugs. But I DO like good-night hugs and kisses—and good-morning ones, too.

It is very important to remember that the usual everyday hugs and kisses and touching and holding hands among family and good friends are perfectly normal. We all need cuddles and hugs and kisses—from our mothers, fathers, grandparents, sisters, brothers, or other family members, or from family friends and good friends—from people we trust and from people who love us.

TALKING ABOUT IT

HIV and AIDS

Chances are you know something about HIV and AIDS. You may have even heard that HIV can have something to do with sex— or with drugs and needles. Wanting to know about HIV and AIDS is perfectly normal. And knowing about them can help to keep people safe from getting HIV and AIDS.

Hearing about HIV and AIDS is scary . . .

Talking about it is scary, too . . .

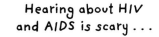

KNOWING ABOUT HIV AND AIDS

HIV is the virus—the germ—that causes AIDS. A virus is a germ that can cause a person to become sick. Most germs—like colds and flus—usually cause people to become sick for only a short time, and then they get better. A person who has HIV may stay well and feel healthy for many years. But when a person who has HIV develops AIDS, he or she may become very sick and may not get better. It is very sad that so many people who have had AIDS have died. But scientists have discovered some medicines that are helping more and more people who have HIV to feel better and live longer. And scientists are working day and night trying to find even better ways to keep people safe from getting HIV and to help people who have HIV. Scientists have also discovered ways people CANNOT get HIV and CAN get HIV.

It says here, "The H in HIV stands for 'human' because the HIV virus is found only in humans—not animals. The V in HIV stands for 'virus.'"

And it says here, "The A in AIDS stands for 'acquired,' which means 'something a person can get.'"

ATTENTION!! SCIENTISTS WORKING DAY AND NIGHT

WAYS A PERSON **CANNOT** GET HIV

- A person *CANNOT* get HIV from going to school or work with a person who has HIV, from playing with a person who has HIV, from hugging a person who has HIV, or from giving a high-five or a kiss hello or good-bye to someone who has HIV.

- A person *CANNOT* get HIV from a cough or a sneeze, or a bug bite, or from sitting on the same toilet seat that someone with HIV has sat on, or from swimming in the same pool with someone who has HIV.

- A person *CANNOT* get HIV from touching blood, saliva, urine, or other body fluids from a person who has HIV.

- A person *CANNOT* get HIV from a brand-new, clean, and germ-free needle that a doctor or nurse uses to give a shot, or from a brand-new, clean, and germ-free needle that is used to pierce ears for earrings.

WAYS A PERSON **CAN** GET HIV

- A person *CAN* get HIV from having sexual intercourse with a person who has HIV. Other infections can also be passed from one person to another during sexual intercourse. When people have sexual intercourse, wearing a condom can help keep a person safe from getting HIV or passing HIV— or some other infections—from one person to another.

- A person *CAN* get HIV from blood that is injected into one's body by drug, tattoo, or ear-piercing needles that have been used by someone who has HIV or by sharing needles. That's because people who are infected with HIV have the virus in their blood. Other infections can be passed from one person to another these same ways. But all blood that is given to people who need blood in a hospital or home is tested before it is given to a person to make sure it does not have HIV or other infections in it.

- If a pregnant woman has HIV, sometimes the virus CAN be passed on to her fetus—and her baby COULD be born with HIV. A pregnant woman who has HIV can take a medicine that can help to keep her baby from being born with HIV. And some babies—but not all—CAN get HIV from their mothers' breast milk if the mother has HIV. Instead, a baby can drink special milk called formula from a bottle.

Talking about it makes me feel better.

Knowing about it makes me feel safer.

People who have HIV, and babies and kids who are born with HIV, often stay well and feel healthy for many years. It's important to treat a person who has been infected with HIV, or who has AIDS, as you would treat any friend. Give a hug, a high-five, or a kiss hello to that person. Play with, hang out with, go to a movie with, or ride bikes with that person—and do the many things you like to do with a good friend.

21

GURGLES AND DROOLS
Feelings about Babies—Fun with Babies

No matter how or when you arrived—or whether you are an only child, the youngest child, a middle child, or the oldest child in your family—you will always have a very special place in your family.

If you are an older brother or sister and there is a new baby in your family, you may have a lot of feelings about the new baby. At times, you may feel happy and even excited.

At other times, you may feel disappointed that the new baby is so small and can't do the kinds of things you can do—like reading books, playing soccer, eating spaghetti, flying a kite, baking cookies, or singing a song.

I sure don't like helping out with those diapers!

I sure don't like it when a baby cries.

Sometimes, you may feel angry at your mother or father for having a new baby, or feel left out or sad. You may wish that your mother or father would be with you instead of the new baby. You may even feel angry at the new baby. And at times, you may not feel like helping out with or taking care of the new baby.

Having any of those feelings about a baby brother or sister, or about a baby cousin, or a friend's baby sister or brother, is perfectly normal. Most kids have these kinds of feelings. But the truth is—babies love to be with older kids. They learn so much by being with older kids like you and watching what you do.

WAYS TO HAVE FUN WITH A BABY

Try whispering, or talking, or even singing to a baby. Try making a silly face. Chances are the baby will love that. Babies love to look at faces most of all. But don't get too close to the baby's face. Babies can get scared and may cry if you do.

When a baby gets tired or bored, the baby will tell you—by turning his or her head away, or crying, or falling asleep. Babies gurgle and drool a lot when you play and talk with them. That means they are having a good time with you. Babies like to have fun.

LET'S CELEBRATE!

Happy Birth Day! Happy Adoption Day!

All around the world, the arrival or adoption of a baby or child is usually one of the most exciting and amazing events ever!

There was a big buzz in my family when I arrived!

There was the biggest flutter in my family when I arrived!

In the United States, many families hang brightly colored balloons or a banner with the words "It's a GIRL!" or "It's a BOY!" outside their house or apartment. Some families put pink or blue ribbons on their front door.

In the highlands of Kenya where the Gusii people live, mothers who have a new baby walk to a place where paths cross. When people walk by, they wish the baby well and give the mother a coin to bring the baby good luck and good health.

In Russia, when a new baby arrives home, the baby is laid on a fur to bring the baby good luck, good health, and wealth.

WE ARE PROUD TO ANNOUNCE BABY ODETTE

BORN ON NOVEMBER 11th 2013

In many countries, families send out cards or letters—often with a photograph—to announce the arrival of a new baby or child.

In the mountains of Switzerland, families hang a toy stork and other baby toys on a pole outside the house to tell everyone that a new baby has arrived.

In Finland, a baby is given a piece of silver—often a spoon—when the baby is one month old. Every year, for the next twelve years, the child is given another piece of silver to celebrate its childhood.

In Lebanon, a special rice pudding with nuts is made by someone in the new baby's family. Everyone who visits the baby eats a spoonful of the pudding to wish the baby good health.

In parts of China, a new baby's parent or parents give eggs that have been dyed red to other family members and friends to celebrate the baby's arrival. The color red stands for happiness, celebration, and good luck.

In Nigeria, eight days after a baby is born, every person who knows the baby's family comes to a ceremony at which the mother and father name the baby.

In Armenia, soon after a baby is home, the baby is given a bracelet with beads—and blue stones that look like eyes—to protect the baby from evil and harm.

In parts of Costa Rica, a baby's family and friends have a potluck dinner at the baby's home, so that the parents do not have to cook any meals for several days.

All around the world, families and friends celebrate the arrival of a baby or child in different ways. But one thing is the same for almost every family: Families love to celebrate because they are so happy and so excited to have a baby or child become part of their family.

IT'S SO AMAZING!
Still Talking!

Thank you to EVERYONE who helped with this book!

And a SPECIAL thank-you to all who helped with this SPECIAL anniversary edition!

Without all of you, we could not have created this newest edition of *It's So Amazing!* Your expertise helped us ensure that this book contains the latest and most accurate information possible, information that answers today's kids' questions and concerns about how boys' and girls' bodies are the same and different, how babies are made, and how kids bodies grow and change. Thank you for teaching us so well.

R. H. H. and M. E.

Wendy Apfel, *educational technology coordinator, Bank Street School for Children, New York, New York*

Deborah Chamberlain, MA, LMHC, *mental health specialist, Cambridge, Massachusetts*

Angela Diaz, MD, MPH, *professor, Department of Pediatrics and Department of Preventive Medicine, Icahn School of Medicine at Mount Sinai; director, Mount Sinai Adolescent Health Center, New York, New York*

Benjamin H. Harris, PhD, *clinical psychologist, Doctoral Program in Clinical Psychology, City College, CUNY, New York, New York*

David B. Harris, PhD, *child advocate, Children's Research and Education Institute, New York, New York*

Emily Harris, MD, *pediatrician, New York, New York*

Hilary Harris, *consultant, New York, New York*

William W. Harris, PhD, *child advocate, Children's Research and Education Institute, New York, New York*

Alexandra M. Harrison, MD, *child psychiatrist, child and adult psychoanalyst, Boston Psychoanalytic Society and Institute; Cambridge Health Alliance, Cambridge, Massachusetts*

Robyn Heilbrun, JD, *consultant, Sausalito, California*

Jennifer Johnsen, MPH, *director of health information, Planned Parenthood Federation of America, New York, New York*

Leslie M. Kantor, MPH, *vice president of education, Planned Parenthood Federation of America, New York, New York; assistant professor, Mailman School of Public Health, Columbia University, New York, New York*

Perri Klass, MD, *professor of journalism and pediatrics, New York University, New York, New York*

Elizabeth A. Levy, *children's book author, New York, New York*

Jay A. Levy, MD, *professor, Department of Medicine, research associate, Cancer Research Institute, University of California School of Medicine, San Francisco, California*

Eli H. Newberger, MD, *pediatrician; founder and medical director, 1970–2000, Child Protection Program; Adjunct in Pediatrics, Boston Children's Hospital; Assistant Professor of Pediatrics, Harvard Medical School, Boston, Massachusetts*

Heather Z. Sankey, MD, *vice chair for education, Department of Obstetrics and Gynecology, Baystate Medical Center, Springfield, Massachusetts*

Annabel Sheinberg, MM, *education director, Planned Parenthood Association of Utah, Salt Lake City, Utah*

A giant thank-you to our editor, **Hilary Van Dusen,** *our designer,* **Nathan Pyritz,** *our art director,* **Chris Paul,** *and* **Miriam Newman,** *for your commitment to keeping this book current for today's kids, no matter how much time and work it took to do so.*

R. H. H. and M. E.

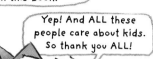

Thank you to ALL these people who ALL helped with this book!

Yep! And ALL these people care about kids. So thank you ALL!

THANK YOU!

Reverend Jory Agate, *Unitarian Universalist Association, Boston, Massachusetts*

Tina Alu, *sexuality education coordinator, Cambridge Family Planning, Cambridge, Massachusetts*

Marie Baratta, *administrator, Cambridge, Massachusetts*

Elizabeth Bartholet, JD, *professor, Harvard Law School, Cambridge, Massachusetts*

Fran Basche, *sexuality education trainer, Watertown, Massachusetts*

Toni Belfield, *Director of Information, The Family Planning Association, London, England*

Emily Berkman, MD, *pediatrician, New York, New York*

Merton Bernfield, MD, *professor of pediatrics, director, Joint Program in Neonatology, Harvard Medical School, Children's Hospital, Boston, Massachusetts*

Sarah Birss, MD, *pediatrician/child psychiatrist, Cambridge, Massachusetts*

Ellysa Stern Cahoy, *children's librarian, Burlington Public Library, Burlington, Massachusetts*

Deborah Chamberlain, MA, LMHC, *mental health specialist, Cambridge, Massachusetts*

David S. Chapin, MD, *director of gynecology, Beth Israel Deaconness Medical Center, Boston, Massachusetts*

Donald J. Cohen, MD, *director, professor of psychiatry, pediatrics, and psychology, Yale University Child Study Center, New Haven, Connecticut*

Eileen Costello, MD, *assistant clinical director of pediatrics, Boston University School of Medicine; pediatrician, Dorchester House, Dorchester, Massachusetts*

Sally Crissman, *science educator, Shady Hill School, Cambridge, Massachusetts*

Angela Diaz, MD, MPH, *professor of pediatrics and community medicine, Mount Sinai School of Medicine; director, Mount Sinai Adolescent Health Center, New York, New York*

Mary Dominguez, *science teacher, Shady Hill School, Cambridge, Massachusetts*

Nancy Drooker, *psychologist and sexuality education consultant, San Francisco, California*

Nicki Nichols Gamble, *past president, Planned Parenthood League of Massachusetts, Boston, Massachusetts*

Hilary Grand, *consultant, New York, New York*

Benjamin H. Harris, PhD, *clinical psychologist, Doctoral Program in Clinical Psychology, City College, CUNY, New York, New York*

David B. Harris, PhD, *child advocate, Children's Research and Educational Institute, New York, New York*

William W. Harris, PhD, *child advocate, Children's Research and Educational Institute, New York, New York*

Gerald Hass, MD, *pediatrician, Cambridge, Massachusetts; physician in chief, South End Community Health Center, Boston, Massachusetts*

Robyn Heilbrun, JD, *consultant, Sausalito, California*

Doris B. Held, MED, *psychotherapist, Harvard Medical School; member of the Governor's Commission on Gay and Lesbian Youth for the Commonwealth of Massachusetts, Cambridge, Massachusetts*

Pat Horn, *teacher, Shady Hill School, Cambridge, Massachusetts*

Michael Iskowitz, *policy and strategy architect, Washington, D.C.*

Suzan Kaitz, *chair, The PURPOSE Campaign, Planned Parenthood League of Massachusetts, Boston, Massachusetts*

Leslie M. Kantor, MPH, *vice president of education, Planned Parenthood Federation of America, New York, New York; assistant professor, Mailman School of Public Health, Columbia University, New York, New York*

Jill Kantrowitz, *director of education, Planned Parenthood League of Massachusetts, Boston, Massachusetts*

Larry Kessler, *executive director, AIDS Action Committee of Massachusetts, Boston, Massachusetts*

Rona Knight, PhD, *child, adolescent, and adult analyst, Newton, Massachusetts*

Philip Kremen, *barrister, London, England*

Robert A. Levine, PhD, *professor of education, human development, and anthropology, Harvard University Graduate School of Education, Cambridge, Massachusetts*

Elizabeth A. Levy, *children's book author, New York, New York*

Jay Levy, MD, *professor, Department of Medicine, research associate, Cancer Research Institute, University of California School of Medicine, San Francisco, California*

Carol Lynch, *director of education and training, Planned Parenthood League of Massachusetts, Boston, Massachusetts*

Steven Marans, PhD, *associate professor of child psychoanalysis, Yale University Child Study Center, New Haven, Connecticut*

Wendy Dalton Marans, MSC, *associate research scientist, Yale University Child Study Center, New Haven, Connecticut*

Kim Marshall, *principal, Mather School, Boston, Massachusetts*

Linda C. Mayes, MD, *associate professor of child psychiatry/pediatrics and psychology, Yale University Child Study Center, New Haven, Connecticut*

Michael McGee, *past vice president for education, Planned Parenthood Federation of America, New York, New York*

Jennifer McGuinn, *teacher, Shady Hill School, Cambridge, Massachusetts*

Ronald James Moglia, EdD, *professor, Department of Health, New York University, New York, New York*

Patricia C. Morris, *teacher, Mather School, Boston, Massachusetts*

Eli H. Newberger, MD, *pediatrician; founder and medical director, 1970–2000, Child Protection Program; Adjunct in Pediatrics, Boston Children's Hospital; Assistant Professor of Pediatrics, Harvard Medical School, Boston, Massachusetts*

June Nichols, RN, *Walpole, Massachusetts*

Jan Paradise, MD, *associate professor of pediatrics, Boston University School of Medicine, Boston, Massachusetts*

Deb Polansky, *teacher, Shady Hill School, Cambridge, Massachusetts*

Gale Pryor, *author, Belmont, Massachusetts*

Jeffrey Pudney, PhD, *research associate, Harvard Medical School, Boston, Massachusetts*

Louise Rice, RN, *director of education, AIDS Action Committee of Massachusetts, Boston, Massachusetts*

Laura Riley, MD, *obstetrician/gynecologist, director, Ob/Gyn Infectious Diseases, Massachusetts General Hospital, Boston, Massachusetts*

Sukey Rosenbaum, *parent, New York, New York*

Deborah M. Rothman, *sexuality educator, author, Baltimore, Maryland*

Heather Z. Sankey, MD, *vice chair for education, Department of Obstetrics and Gynecology, Baystate Medical Center, Springfield, Massachusetts*

Hermine Sarkissian, *pediatrician, Yerevan, Armenia*

Deborah Schoeberlein, *director, Redefining Actions & Decisions Educational Programs, Carbondale, Colorado*

Carol Sepkoski, PhD, *developmental psychologist, Cambridge, Massachusetts*

Deidre Sheedy, *parent, Concord, Massachusetts*

Rachel Skvirsky, PhD, *associate professor of biology, University of Massachusetts, Boston, Massachusetts*

Catherine Steiner-Adair, PhD, *psychologist, Lexington, Massachusetts*

Julie Stevenson, *teacher, The San Francisco School, San Francisco, California*

Michael G. Thompson, PhD, *clinical psychologist, author, Cambridge, Massachusetts*

Trish Moylan Torruella, MPH, *sexuality education consultant, New York, New York*

Edward Z. Tronick, PhD, *distinguished university professor of psychology, College of Liberal Arts; director, Child Development Unit, University of Massachusetts, Boston, Massachusetts*

Susan Webber, *consultant, Arlington, Massachusetts*

Barry Zuckerman, MD, *Department of Pediatrics, Boston University School of Medicine, Boston City Hospital, Boston, Massachusetts*

Pamela Meyer Zuckerman, MD, *pediatrician, Brookline, Massachusetts*

Thanks to all our colleagues at Candlewick Press and Walker Books. And a very special thanks to **Amy Ehrlich, Liz Gavril, Julie Bushway, Anne Moore, Gill Willis, Wendy Boase, Mary Lee Donovan, Jamie Michalak, Jeff Fresenius,** *and* **Ruth Williams.**

R. H. H. and M. E.

INDEX

There are so-ooo many A-MAZING things in this book! And right here is a list of all those things—with their page numbers—so you can find out WHAT you want to find out.

One last thing. The BOLD numbers are the page numbers WHERE you can find out what a word means!

INDEX

It's NOT the Stork!

"An amazingly clear and comprehensive . . . introductory course on the birds and bees. This must-have family resource . . . is reassuring, accurate, up-to-date, and age-appropriate." —*San Francisco Chronicle*

For age 4 and up

It's So Amazing!

"Even if your child hasn't reached puberty, talk with him or her about what lies ahead. . . . *It's So Amazing!* . . . could help prepare your son or daughter—as well as reassure you."

—*Time* Magazine

For age 7 and up

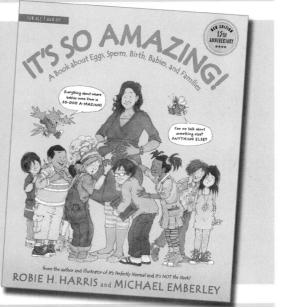

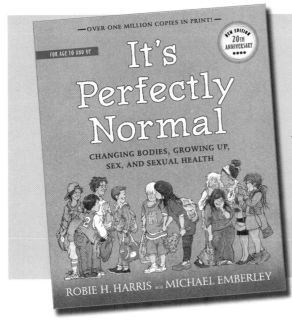

It's Perfectly Normal

★ "A wonderful guide for young adolescents setting sail on the stormy seas of puberty."
—*School Library Journal* (starred review)

For age 10 and up

Here's what people are saying about the series

"The simple words and pictures help parents answer young children's questions clearly and comfortably." – T. Berry Brazelton, MD, founder of the Brazelton Touchpoints Center, Children's Hospital, Boston, and **Joshua Sparrow, MD**, co-authors of *Touchpoints: Birth to Three* and *Touchpoints: Three to Six*

"Will answer questions, start conversations, and make everyone smile."
– **Perri Klass, MD**, Professor of Journalism and Pediatrics, New York University; Director of Graduate Studies, Arthur L. Carter Journalism Institute

Check out all the books in the series

Who Has What? ALL About Girls' Bodies and Boys' Bodies
ROBIE H. HARRIS
illustrated by NADINE BERNARD WESTCOTT

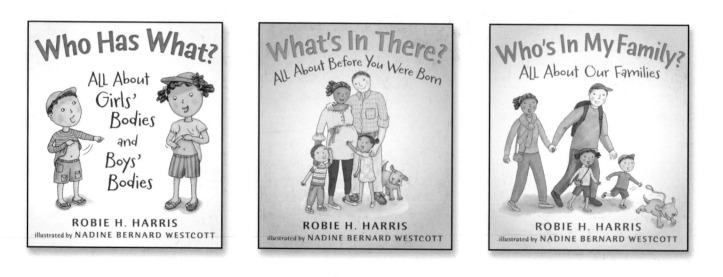

What's In There? ALL About Before You Were Born
ROBIE H. HARRIS
illustrated by NADINE BERNARD WESTCOTT

Who's In My Family? ALL About Our Families
ROBIE H. HARRIS
illustrated by NADINE BERNARD WESTCOTT

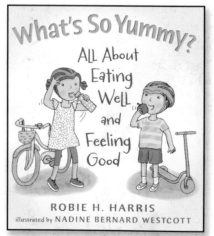

What's So Yummy? ALL About Eating Well and Feeling Good
ROBIE H. HARRIS
illustrated by NADINE BERNARD WESTCOTT

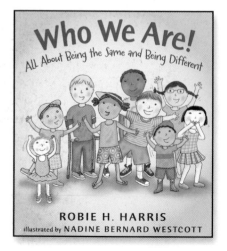

Who We Are! ALL About Being the Same and Being Different
ROBIE H. HARRIS
illustrated by NADINE BERNARD WESTCOTT